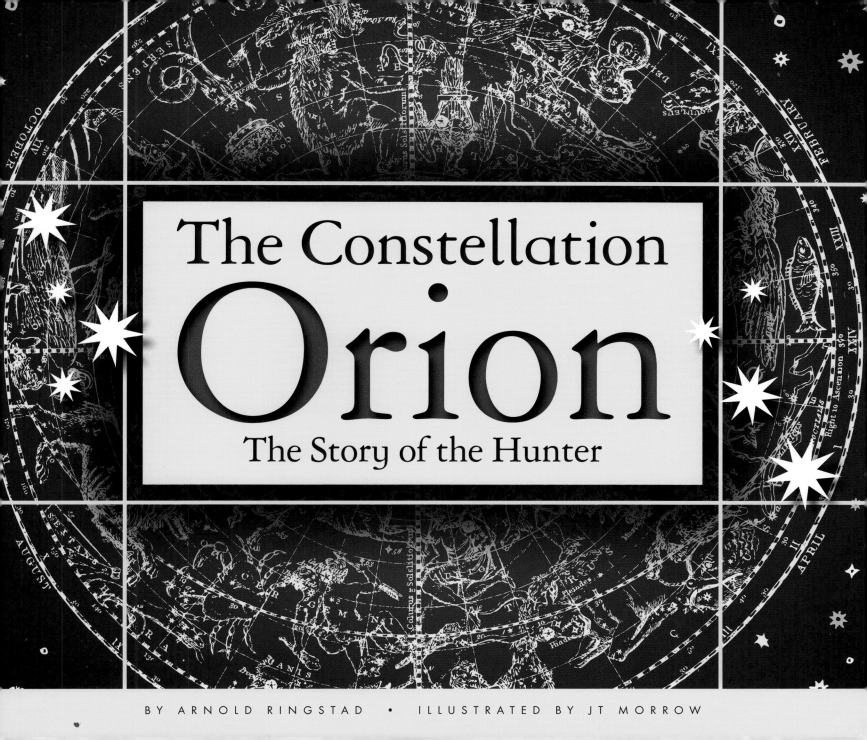

The Constellation
Orion
The Story of the Hunter

BY ARNOLD RINGSTAD • ILLUSTRATED BY JT MORROW

The Child's World

Published by The Child's World®
1980 Lookout Drive • Mankato, MN 56003-1705
800-599-READ • www.childsworld.com

Acknowledgments
The Child's World®: Mary Berendes, Publishing Director
Red Line Editorial: Editorial direction and production
The Design Lab: Design

Photographs ©: US Naval Observatory Library, 5; Anna-Julia/
Shutterstock Images, 6; EpicStockMedia/Shutterstock Images, 7; Santia/
Shutterstock Images, 9; Mironov/Shutterstock Images, 10; NASA, 11; Bill
Frische/Shutterstock Images, 11; Bridgeman Art Library/Getty Images,
13; Telesniuk/Shutterstock Images, 15; Georgy Markov/Shutterstock
Images, 16; Kris Black/iStockphoto, 17; Peresanz/Shutterstock Images,
27

Design elements: Alisafoytik/Dreamstime

ISBN: 9781623234874
LCCN: 2013931358

Printed in the United States of America
Mankato, MN
July, 2013
PA02168

ABOUT THE AUTHOR

Arnold Ringstad lives in Minnesota.
He loves looking into the night sky
with his telescope.

ABOUT THE ILLUSTRATOR

JT Morrow has worked as a freelance
illustrator for more than 20 years and has
won several awards. He also works in
graphic design and animation. Morrow
lives just south of San Francisco, California,
with his wife and daughter.

Table of Contents

CHAPTER 1

The Constellation Orion

A fearsome hunter lives in the night sky. He carries a heavy club and a strong shield. It is difficult to see him at first. Use your imagination, and he comes into view. Three bright stars make up his belt. Two stars above the belt are his shoulders. Two stars below it are his legs. Above his right shoulder rises a group of stars. These show his powerful club. Near his left shoulder is another line of stars. These make up his arm and mighty shield. This hunter's name is Orion.

In some pictures, Orion holds an animal skin instead of a shield.

What Is a Star?

During the day, we can see one star. It is the Sun. The Sun is the closest star to Earth. But on a clear night, we can see thousands of stars. Like our Sun, stars are huge, bright objects. They give off light and heat. However, they are so far away from us that they look like tiny bright specks. The nearest star is about 24,900,000,000,000 (24.9 trillion) miles from Earth. Imagine the Sun were the size of a baseball. The nearest star would be more than 1,300 miles (2,000 km) away! Most stars are even farther away!

▲ We see the Sun rise and set each day because Earth spins. Night is when your part of the planet is turned away from the Sun.

The stars you can see are located in our **galaxy**. A galaxy is an enormous group of stars. It is held together by **gravity**. Our galaxy is called the Milky Way. It is named for the way the galaxy looks from Earth. It appears as a milky band of light in the sky.

There are many galaxies out there. They are very faint and hard to see. You need a telescope to see most of them. Galaxies are so far away it is difficult to imagine the distance. The nearest is about 14,600,000,000,000,000,000 (14.6 quintillion) miles from Earth! It would take a car almost 280,000,000,000,000 (280 trillion) years to drive that far. That's more than 2,000 times as old as the **universe**.

▼ The Milky Way stretches across the night sky.

Stars in Orion

Orion's belt has three stars. From left to right, they are named Alnitak, Alnilam, and Mintaka. Four stars surround the belt, one at each corner. They make up the shoulders and legs of Orion. Above and to the left of the belt is Betelgeuse. Betelgeuse has a reddish color. It is the second-brightest star in Orion. It is one of the brightest stars in the sky. It makes up the hunter's right shoulder. Betelgeuse is nearly 1,000 times larger than our Sun.

The star Bellatrix is above and to the right of the belt. It has a pale yellow color. Below and to the right is Rigel, a bluish star. Rigel is the brightest star in Orion. Below and to the left is the star Saiph.

STAR SIZES
The largest star that **astronomers** know of is VY Canis Majoris. It is found in the Canis Major constellation near Orion. Astronomers think the star could be 2,000 times larger than our Sun.

Betelgeuse

Bellatrix

Mintaka

Alnitak   Alnilam

Rigel

Saiph

► *Do you see how Orion's stars make the shape of a man? What other patterns do you see?*

Deep Space Objects

In addition to its stars, Orion also has deep space objects. These are objects in distant space that are not individual stars. They include galaxies and other groups of stars. **Nebulae** are one type of distant body. The Orion Nebula and the Horsehead Nebula are both visible in Orion. Through a powerful telescope, they look like glowing clouds.

The Orion Nebula is located just below Orion's belt. It can be seen faintly with the naked eye. It is much easier to see through a telescope. The Orion Nebula has a group of four enormous stars. These four stars are surrounded by hundreds of smaller ones. The light from the stars makes the nebula glow.

▲ *The Orion Nebula glows purple in this telescope's image.*

▶ *Opposite page bottom: The Horsehead Nebula*

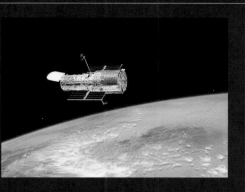

▲ *Hubble Space Telescope*

SEEING DEEP INTO SPACE

We need powerful telescopes to see deep space objects such as nebulae. One powerful telescope is the Hubble Space Telescope. It was launched into space in 1990 by the space shuttle *Discovery*. It orbits around Earth, taking pictures of space and sending them to Earth for study. The telescope is about the size of a school bus. Its main mirror is 94 inches (240 cm) across. The Hubble Space Telescope has given astronomers amazingly clear views of stars, galaxies, and deep space objects.

The Horsehead Nebula is also located below Orion's belt. It contains stars surrounded by a large cloud of gas and dust. The stars light up the gas. This gives part of the nebula a colorful appearance. The dust blocks the light from the stars. This makes another part of the nebula dark. The darkened area looks a bit like a horse's head.

CHAPTER 2

The Origin of the Myth of Orion

The ancient Sumerians first identified Orion. These people lived more than 5,000 years ago in the Middle East. The Sumerians saw their **legendary** hero Gilgamesh in the constellation. They saw Gilgamesh battling another constellation. This was the Bull of Heaven, a character from Sumerian mythology. The Greeks knew this constellation as the bull Taurus.

▶ Opposite page: Orion and Taurus fight in this constellation map from the 1700s.

13

Orion and the Greeks

The ancient Greeks saw their own stories and heroes when they looked up at the stars. They replaced Gilgamesh with Orion. Orion was the son of a god and a human woman. His father was Poseidon, the Greek sea god. He gave Orion the power to walk on water. His mother was Euryale. She was the daughter of King Minos, from the Greek island of Crete. Orion was a giant hunter who carried a powerful club.

The Greeks linked other constellations with Orion. His hunting dogs follow him through the sky. These are the constellations Canis Major and Canis Minor. On the opposite side of the sky is the scorpion Scorpius. Scorpius was Orion's enemy.

▶ *Opposite page: The sea god Poseidon gave Orion special powers.*

The earliest ancient Greeks knew the Orion constellation. The epic poet Homer wrote about Orion, Canis Major, and Canis Minor in a poem. In another poem, he mentions the hero Orion. Homer describes him as a handsome warrior. In this poem, Orion's club is made of bronze that cannot break.

▲ Homer wrote about Orion i famous poems.

Ptolemy

Astronomer Ptolemy lived in Alexandria in Egypt between 100 and 200 AD. He wrote about 48 standard constellations. His constellations are almost the same as our constellations today. Orion is one of the constellations in his original list.

► Orion is near Canis Major in the sky.

Orion ►

Canis Major ►

CHAPTER 3
The Story of Orion

Long ago, the great hunter Orion visited the island of Chios. He met the island's ruler, King Oenopion. When greeting the king, Orion spotted the king's daughter, Merope. Merope was very beautiful. Orion immediately fell in love with her. He would do everything he could to win her love. He came up with a plan. He would convince the king to let him marry Merope.

Orion decided to use his legendary hunting skills. He would destroy all the wild beasts on Chios. For days he ran around the island with his bronze club. He cleared the island of animals. After he finished, he returned to King Oenopion. Still the king refused to let Orion marry his daughter. But Orion would not give up. The king was furious that the hunter would not leave. King Oenopion decided to punish Orion for pursuing his daughter.

King Oenopion sneaked into Orion's room while he slept. In one quick motion, he took out Orion's eyes. This would prevent Orion from seeing Merope again. The king then **banished** Orion from Chios. He sent the depressed Orion out to sea. Fortunately, Orion had the power to walk on water. He began traveling northward from the island.

Eventually, Orion heard the faint sound of a hammer in the distance. He followed the sound. He finally reached the island of Lemnos. This was more than 100 miles (160 km) north of Chios. Lemnos was home to the **forge** of Hephaestus. Hephaestus was the Greek god of fire. The hammering sound was made by the Cyclopes. These were giant one-eyed monsters that worked for Hephaestus at his forge.

Orion met the god Hephaestus at his forge. Hephaestus took pity on the blinded Orion. The god decided to help him. He thought for a minute and then called for an assistant, Cedalion. Hephaestus told Cedalion to climb up onto Orion's shoulders. Cedalion would act as Orion's new eyes. He would tell Orion what was happening around him. Orion was grateful for Hephaestus's kindness and Cedalion's help.

He thanked Hephaestus and left the forge, carrying Cedalion on his broad shoulders. After leaving Hephaestus, Orion walked east. It was still the middle of the night. But soon the Sun began to rise. Its golden rays struck Orion's eyes. He saw a flash, and his sight was restored!

The legends do not agree how Orion died. In one story, Orion is proud and boastful. One day, Orion said he was the best hunter ever. He declared that he could kill any beast on Earth. Artemis, the goddess of hunting, did not like his boasting. She summoned a tiny scorpion. The scorpion stung Orion, killing him. Orion was then placed in the night sky. He is far away from Scorpius, the scorpion constellation.

In another story, love is Orion's downfall. One day while hunting, Orion met the goddess Artemis. They started hunting together. Soon they fell in love. But Apollo, Artemis's brother, did not want them to marry. Apollo made a plan to kill Orion. Apollo and Artemis went walking along a beach. Orion was swimming far from shore. Artemis did not know he was there, but Apollo did. Apollo pointed out a small object floating far away in the water. He bet his sister she could not hit it with an arrow. She fired the arrow and scored a direct hit. She swam out to see what she hit. It was Orion! Artemis's arrow had killed him. She was very sad. So she placed Orion in the night sky among the other constellations.

CHAPTER 4

Orion in Other Cultures

People around the world told their own stories about patterns in the night sky. The things they saw in the stars did not usually match what people in different places saw. However, very rarely, constellations from different cultures were similar. This happened with Orion and the Chinese hero Shen. *Shen* means "three stars," referring to the three stars of Orion's belt.

Like Orion, Shen is a great hunter and warrior. He has ten stars: four stars in his outline, three in his belt, and three in his sword. Orion's other stars are parts of different Chinese constellations. The ten stars also represent the generals Shen led.

▶ People around the world have made up stories about the three bright stars in Orion's belt.

CHAPTER 5

How to Find Orion

Orion is one of the easiest constellations to find. Look for the three bright stars that make his belt. Search in the southwest sky if you live in the Northern **Hemisphere**. Orion can be seen during winter and early spring. Look to the northwest sky if you live in the Southern Hemisphere. In the Southern Hemisphere, Orion appears upside down. Near the equator, Orion appears in the western sky.

▶ *Opposite page: Look for the three stars of Orion's belt to find the constellation.*

Glossary

astronomers (uh-STRAW-nuh-murz)
Scientists who study stars and other objects in space are called astronomers. Astronomers study Orion.

banished (BAN-ishd)
A person who is banished is forced to leave a place. Orion was banished from the island Chios.

epic (EP-ik)
A long story in the form of a poem, usually describing the adventures of a hero, is an epic. The Sumerians wrote an epic about their hero, Gilgamesh.

forge (FORJ)
A forge is a blacksmith's workshop. The god Hephaestus made tools in his forge.

galaxy (GAL-ax-ee)
A group of millions or billions of stars form a galaxy. Our galaxy is called the Milky Way.

gravity (GRAV-uh-tee)
Gravity is a force that pulls objects toward each other. Gravity pulls stars together.

hemisphere (HEM-uh-spheer)
One half of a planet is one hemisphere. You can see Orion from the Northern Hemisphere.

legendary (LEJ-uhn-der-ee)
If something is legendary it comes from a story handed down from the past. Stories about Orion are legendary.

mythological (mith-oh-LAW-jik-uhl)
Mythological means coming from a culture's set of stories or beliefs. Many constellations are based on mythological stories.

nebulae (NEB-you-lay)
Nebulae are clouds of gas and dust in space. There are two nebulae in the constellation Orion.

rural (RUR-uhl)
Rural means coming from the country rather than a city. Rural ancient Greeks worshipped the goddess Artemis.

universe (YOU-nih-verse)
The universe is everything that exists in space. The universe is huge and filled with stars.

Learn More

Books

Galat, Joan Marie. *Dot to Dot in the Sky: Stories in the Stars*. North Vancouver, BC: Whitecap Books, 2003.

Peters, Stephanie True. *Library of Constellations: Orion*. New York: PowerKids Press, 2003.

Wagner, Kathi. *The Everything Kids' Astronomy Book*. Avon, MA: Adams Media, 2008.

Web Sites

Visit our Web site for links about Orion:

childsworld.com/links

Note to Parents, Teachers, and Librarians:
We routinely verify our Web links to make sure they are safe and active sites. So encourage your readers to check them out!

Index